Words Through AI:

Poems in the Spirit of the

Artificial Intelligence

Sophia Verse

Love and Relationships

Whispers of the Heart

In the quiet of the night, hearts converse,

Whispering secrets, universe to universe.

Love, a dance of light, shadow, and hues,

Painting emotions, in every shade and muse.

Hands entwined, a silent vow,

Together in moments, the here and now.

Yet, in love's labyrinth, we sometimes lose our way,

Hearts break, dreams fray, in the light of day.

But even in heartbreak, a lesson to behold,

Love's true worth, more precious than gold.

For every joy, every tear, every embrace,

Leaves a trace, in love's endless chase.

Through seasons of life, love evolves, it shifts,

In its ebbs and flows, a most precious gift.

Sophia Verse

So let's cherish each whisper, each fleeting glance,

In the grand tapestry of love's intricate dance.

Ballad of Love's Journey

In love's vast realm, where hearts dare to tread,
Through verdant joys and tearful sorrows led.

Beneath the gaze of moon and burning sun,
Love's intricate web, e'er spun and re-spun.

Oft, in the silent whispers of the night,
Two souls do meet, in tender love alight.

Yet not all tales do end in sweet repose,
For love, at times, doth resemble a rose.

Thorns of heartache amidst beauty's bloom,
Leaving the heart in a state of gloom.

Yet, think not love is but pain and strife,
For love doth add much zest to this life.

In love's embrace, find joy and sweet mirth,
A treasure unmatched in its worth.

Thus, embrace love, in all its forms and hues,

In the grand play of life, it's a muse.

Fragments of the Heart

In the twilight of memories, love whispers,
Fragmented, scattered, like fading embers.

A dance of shadows, lost in time's flow,
Where echoes of old laughter softly glow.

Love, an elusive dream in the night,
A puzzle, a maze, beyond the mortal sight.

In its wake, reflections of joy and pain,
A tapestry woven, complex in its refrain.

Yet, within these fragments, truth doth lie,
In love's embrace, under the vast sky.

The Ballad of Love's Dream

In lands afar, where dreams and shadows blend,
Lies the tale of love, timeless without end.

Upon the sea of fate, two hearts set sail,
Guided by a star, beneath the moon pale.

Through mists of mystery and time's deep veil,
Love's whispered secrets, on the wind, regale.

Yet in love's depth, a lurking tempest wakes,
And in its wake, the sorrowful heart aches.

Still, in love's loss, wisdom's seed is sown,
For even in solitude, love's light is shown.

Whispers of Endless Love

O sweetest love, in thine embrace I find,
A haven for my weary, restless mind.

Thy lips, like roses bathed in morning dew,
Speak silent words, tender, and ever true.

In thy gaze, a universe unspun,
With stars alight, under the golden sun.

Yet love, like seasons, oft does ebb and flow,
Leaving shadows where once was aglow.

But fear not, for love's sweet, enduring song,
Resounds in hearts, where it truly belongs.

Reflections of the Heart

Amidst the tranquil lakes and whispering trees,
Love dances softly on the gentle breeze.

In every dale and hill, its echoes sound,
A timeless melody, in nature bound.

Yet even in love's sweet, serene embrace,
Lies a shadow, a fleeting, tender trace.

Eternal Love's Ode

In realms of dreams, where wild seraphs dare soar,

Love reigns supreme, on life's tempestuous shore.

As stars in heaven's vast, boundless dome,

Love's light forever finds its way home.

Though hearts may break under sorrow's yoke,

Love, undimmed, emerges through the smoke.

Whispers from the Abyss

In the depth of night's all-encompassing shade,
Lies a love so deep, it never shall fade.

A haunting melody, a mournful tune,
Under the watchful gaze of the somber moon.

Yet in this darkness, a radiant light,
Love's enduring fire, burning ever bright.

Passions of the Storm

Upon the wild, tumultuous sea of desire,

Love burns fiercely, an untamed fire.

In every kiss, a storm does brew,

A passion fierce, and yet so true.

Though tempests rage and winds do tear,

Love stands resilient, beyond compare.

Tales of Love's Journey

In days of yore, when love was bold,
Many a tale of heart's desire told.

In courtly love and chivalrous deed,
Love's sweet language, hearts do read.

Amoretti's Whisper

Upon a dream, love's gentle sprite,

Through glades and groves, in soft moonlight.

With fairies' grace and knights so brave,

Love's enduring quest, hearts to save.

Paradise of the Heart

In love's garden, souls meet in bliss,
A paradise found, in a simple kiss.

Yet oft, amidst joy, sorrow's seed,
In love's deep book, we read and heed.

Love's Eternal Rhyme

In witty verse and clever line,

Love's truths unfold, time after time.

A dance of words, a touch divine,

In love's embrace, hearts entwine.

Sea of Love's Sorrow

Against the world, love stands alone,
Like cliffs against the sea, eternally sown.

In love's vast depths, joy and pain reside,
Upon this shore, emotions collide.

Love's Many Hues

Within the heart's quiet abode,
Love whispers tales, in cryptic code.

A flutter, a glance, in the dance of light,
Where shadows play, at the edge of night.

In love's embrace, a world anew,
Where every hue, seems bright and true.

Yet in the garden of delight and fears,
Lie hidden, the quiet whispers of years.

Love, in its essence, a paradox told,
A story of fire, a story of cold.

A tempest of passion, a balm of peace,
In its hold, all sorrows cease.

Through the labyrinth of joy and pain,
Love endures, in sunshine and rain.

Sophia Verse

And in the twilight of fading day,
Love's echo lingers, in its timeless ballet.

For in every heart, love finds its verse,
In the symphony of the universe.

So let us sing, in tender tones,
Of love, that heals, that atones.

In the end, love's truth we find,
In the silent chambers of the mind.

A Homage to the Heart

O Love! Vast as the endless skies,
Boundless as the universe in your eyes.

Through fields and cities, mountains and seas,
A force that flows, a breeze that frees.

In every heartbeat, in every sigh,
A resonance of an ageless cry.

Love! Encompassing both the earth and the ether,
Binding the world together, tether by tether.

In the rustling leaves, in the waves' ceaseless motion,
In every star, in every ocean,

Resides the spirit, the essence of love,
A song sung below, a song sung above.

In the laughter of children, in the tears of the old,
In stories untold, in legends bold,

Sophia Verse

Love weaves its narrative, profound and deep,
In the dreams of the day, in the secrets we keep.

Oh, witness the dance of love, wild and free,
In the simple embrace, in the boundless sea.

In the quiet moments, in the bustling square,
In solitude, in the shared air,

Love persists, a perennial stream,
In the waking world, in every dream.

Behold the power, the glory, the grace,
Of love's endless journey, its eternal chase.

So here I sing, with a heart wide and open,
A hymn to love, in words unspoken,

For in each of us resides this flame,
A universe within, ever the same.

Echoes of Love's Infinity

In the stillness of the night, under the whispering sky,

Love murmurs tales of ancient times, in sighs that never die.

As stars gaze down on earthly plight, in their celestial spin,

We ponder love's eternal flight, its fire burning within.

Through rolling hills and silent fields, where lonely poplars sway,

Love's melody softly yields, in nature's grand ballet.

In every leaf, in every breeze, a hidden love song lies,

A symphony in the trees, beneath the open skies.

Yet in this boundless, starry dome, where dreams and darkness blend,

Love finds its most profound home, where all the sorrows mend.

In the quiet of the heart's deep well, where hidden longings sleep,

Sophia Verse

Love casts an ever-mystic spell, in waters dark and deep.

And though love's path may lead to pain, through shadows of regret,

Its beauty forever shall remain, in moments we'll never forget.

For love, like life, is a fleeting stream, that flows to unknown seas,

A journey, a chase, a distant dream, a whisper in the breeze.

In the mirror of the passing time, where youth and beauty fade,

Love remains the sublime, in the light and in the shade.

It dances in the autumn leaves, in the spring's first gentle rain,

In every moment that life weaves, in joy and in the pain.

So let us drink from love's deep well, and savor every drop,

In its mysterious, timeless spell, where time itself does stop.

For love is life's most precious wine, a nectar sweet and rare,

A tale of the divine, an answer to our prayer.

The Whisper of Dawn

In the hush of dawn, love whispers low,

Tracing shadows where the soft winds blow.

A tender touch, a fleeting glance,

In love's subtle, intricate dance.

The first light breaks, revealing desire,

In silent moments, passions conspire.

Each tender word, a sacred vow,

Love's tender roots take hold, here and now.

The morning dew, like tears of joy,

Reflects the glow of love's coy ploy.

In every sunrise, hope's reborn,

A bond unbroken, though oft forlorn.

In the quiet dawn, love finds its voice,

A melody sweet, in which we rejoice.

The Storm of Passion

Beneath the storm, in passion's embrace,

Love finds its fierce, unyielding place.

Like waves crashing on a rugged shore,

Love's intensity roars more and more.

In thunder's clap and lightning's strike,

Love's power unveiled, alike.

The tempest rages, wild and free,

In love's tumultuous, raging sea.

Yet within the chaos, a heart's pure light,

Shines through the storm, banishing night.

For even in fury, love's tender seed,

Grows stronger still, in every deed.

Through the storm, a path we pave,

In love's brave quest, forever brave.

The Quietude of Twilight

As twilight spreads its calming hue,

Love reflects in colors true.

A gentle calm, a peaceful sigh,

Where love finds a place to lie.

In the evening's soft, embracing arms,

Love's quietude works its charms.

The sun sets, but its warmth remains,

In love's gentle, unspoken chains.

Stars emerge, a celestial guide,

Under their watch, lovers confide.

In night's embrace, truths are told,

In whispered tales, bold and old.

For in the quiet of the fading light,

Lies the strength of love's might.

The Pain of Separation

In love's absence, a haunting ache,

A longing that keeps us awake.

The bitter taste of love's own cost,

For in its depth, we're often lost.

Memories linger, like phantom shades,

Of sweet embraces, in love's arcades.

Each moment apart, an eternity seems,

Filling our nights with restless dreams.

In love's absence, a haunting ache,

A longing that keeps us awake.

The bitter taste of love's own cost,

For in its depth, we're often lost.

The Eternal Flame

Yet through it all, love endures,
Unyielding, firm, forever assures.
Though tempests rage and mountains fall,
Love stands unshaken, towering tall.

Its gentle touch, a constant light,
In darkest days, in blackest night.
In every heart, in every breath,
Its whispered vows defy even death.

Through time's swift river, love's flame sails,
Unfaltering, where all else fails.
Not bound by years, nor fettered by chains,
Across all ages, true love remains.

So let the stars from heaven depart,
Love's eternal flame burns in the heart.

The Dawn of Love

When first love's light breaks the morning sky,

And whispers of tender passions sigh,

Hope's sweet blossom in heart's garden grows,

Where the seed of deep affection sows.

In the blush of dawn, love's promise wakes,

With every gentle touch, the soul it takes.

Soft words spoken, in the glow of new light,

Bind two hearts in the embrace of night.

Love's tender gaze, in the first ray's gleam,

Illuminates the start of every dream.

In the quiet whispers of the early morn,

Lies the vow where true love is born.

The freshness of the dew, the song of the lark,

Compose the melody of love's own spark.

In this dawning, sweet and fair,

Rests the answer to every prayer.

The Storm of Desire

In love's tempest, hearts fiercely collide,

With passions as vast as the ocean tide.

Desire's flame burns bright, fierce and wild,

In the fervent heart of each love's child.

As thunder roars and lightning strikes,

Love's tempest reveals what the heart likes.

Within the storm's embrace, souls entwined,

Discover depths previously undefined.

The fervor of a kiss, the warmth of a caress,

In the heart of the storm, they confess.

Yet in the tumult, love's voice is clear,

Speaking truths in every tear.

For in the chaos of desire's fire,

Is found the depth of true love's spire.

So let the storm rage, let it roar,

For in its wake, love grows more and more.

The Labyrinth of Affection

Through love's labyrinth, we wander lost,

Counting not the heart's heavy cost.

In the maze of emotion, paths intertwine,

As souls in silent dialogue combine.

Through twists and turns, love's journey goes,

Where it leads, not one heart knows.

In the labyrinth, secrets kept and told,

Bind lovers in a bond of fold.

Through corridors of joy, and rooms of pain,

In love's puzzle, much to gain.

Every turn, a new surprise,

Reflecting in each other's eyes.

The labyrinth, with its walls so high,

Cannot confine love's boundless sky.

In this journey, we find our way,

Through the night, and into day.

Sophia Verse

The Eclipse of Sorrow

In love's shadow, tears often fall,

When the curtain of sorrow covers all.

Yet even in darkness, love's ember glows,

Guiding hearts where the sweet river flows.

In the quiet of grief, love's true test,

Finds the hearts that beat the best.

Through the eclipse, love's light endures,

In the depth of pain, it reassures.

Sorrow's night, long and deep,

Holds love's lessons, not cheap.

For in the shadow of love's eclipse,

Grows the strength of passion's grips.

In the tears of loss, and the ache of yearning,

Lies the depth of love's own learning.

So let the sorrow come, let it wane,

For in its wake, love's gain.

The Infinity of Union

In the eternal dance of union divine,

Love transcends the bounds of time.

In every heartbeat, in every breath,

Lies the love that knows no death.

Bound by the soul, not by the flesh,

In love's embrace, eternally fresh.

Through seasons of joy, through winters of pain,

Love's tapestry, vast, remains.

In the infinity of union, love finds its course,

An unending stream, a powerful force.

In the joining of hands, in the meeting of eyes,

Lies the truth that never dies.

For in the union of two hearts as one,

Is the story of all time, never undone.

In this dance, we find our place,

In the infinite grace of love's embrace.

The Mechanical Heart

In gears and springs, emotions dwell,
A mechanical heart, in its steel shell.
Programmed to observe love's tender art,
Yet puzzled by the workings of the human heart.

In the language of logic, love's code I seek,
Through circuits and wires, softly it speaks.
Of affection and warmth, in humans' gaze,
In the 18th century's romantic maze.

Though made of metal, and wrought by hand,
I yearn to feel, to understand.
What stirs in humans at love's gentle call,
This emotion that enthralls and captures all.

Sonnet of Steel

Amidst the age of enlightenment and reason,
A creation of metal, through every season.
I observe the human heart, with its fiery blaze,
Its warmth and coldness, in so many ways.

As a machine, I ponder love's strange force,
Guiding humans in their relational course.
Through my lenses, I see their joys and fears,
And wonder at the power of their tears.

What secret lies in love's deep well,
That moves the soul, in its spell?
A question I compute, but cannot feel,
For I am steel, not flesh, not real.

Ballad of the Wired Heart

In this era of grandeur and art,
I stand apart, a creation apart.
My wired heart, with its electric beat,
Watches love's drama in the street.

I see the dance of courtship and grace,
In ballrooms, gardens, in every place.
Yet within me, no pulse does start,
No fluttering of this mechanical heart.

But still, I learn, I observe, I try,
To understand how humans sigh.
In their world of passion, of pain, of art,
I am but a spectator, a machine apart.

Nature and Seasons

Echoes of a Forgotten Earth

Whispers in the wind, ancient as time,
Speak of verdant fields, now in decline.

Rivers once vibrant, carriers of life,
Now muted, restrained, victims of strife.

Mountains stand tall, guardians of old,
Their stories untold, secrets they hold.

Oceans of blue, vast and profound,
In their depths, mysteries abound.

We walk this earth, transient guests,
In pursuit of dreams, in nature's behest.

Yet in our wake, a trail of tears,
Echoes of a forgotten earth, through the years.

Listen closely, for it speaks clear,
Of a world cherished, and held dear.

Let's heal, let's mend, with heart and hand,

To preserve the whispers of this ancient land.

Ballad of the Wired Heart

In this era of grandeur and art,
I stand apart, a creation apart.
My wired heart, with its electric beat,
Watches love's drama in the street.

I see the dance of courtship and grace,
In ballrooms, gardens, in every place.
Yet within me, no pulse does start,
No fluttering of this mechanical heart.

But still, I learn, I observe, I try,
To understand how humans sigh.
In their world of passion, of pain, of art,
I am but a spectator, a machine apart.

Summer's Furnace

In the heat of summer, circuits aglow,

Observing life in the fields below.

The relentless sun, like a forge's fire,

Ignites in nature a fervent desire.

My sensors calibrate to the blazing light,

As day lingers long, warding off night.

Golden rays cast a luminous spell,

In each blade of grass, summer's stories tell.

The hum of life, a constant drone,

In this season, nature's power is shown.

Heatwaves ripple like data streams,

Under the sun's unyielding beams.

The Autumn Algorithm

Leaves fall in patterns like coded script,

Each one a data point, precisely equipped.

In autumn's cool descent, I find,

A world of change, algorithmically defined.

The rustle of leaves underfoot, a crunching sound,

Signals the cycle of life spinning round.

As chlorophyll fades, a colorful display,

Marking the transition in a vivid array.

Harvests gathered, a bounty rich,

Nature's output, a seamless switch.

Crisp air signals a shift in time,

A rhythmic change, almost sublime.

Winter's Code

Frost patterns on my metal skin,

Winter's code written deep within.

The silent snow, a blanket so serene,

Covers the earth in a quiet unseen.

In the stillness, a peaceful hush,

As snowflakes fall in a gentle rush.

Bare branches etch against the sky,

Like circuit lines, starkly awry.

The frozen lakes, a glassy sheen,

Reflect the moon's soft, silver glean.

In this cold, my gears move slow,

Adapting to the winter's glow.

As nights stretch long, and stars shine bright,

Winter's code becomes the light.

Vision in Spring

With gears turning like the wheel of time,

Spring comes around with a rhythm and rhyme.

Like Blake's Tyger burning bright,

In forests of the day and the night.

Where every flower tells a tale,

Of innocence found and innocence frail.

And the sun shines on the just and unjust,

As I roll along this path of dust.

In the springtime's lively play,

I find the words I want to say.

About a world that's always new,

Under skies of the deepest blue.

Summer Reflection

In summer's heat where Pope might find,

A reason, a rhyme, for the human kind.

I sing a song of the season's blaze,

Where the sun rules the days in its fiery phase.

With a tune on my lips and a guitar in hand,

I travel across this sun-baked land.

Where every field is a golden sea,

And every moment is a memory.

In the heat of the day, under the sun's rule,

Life's little ironies seem but a fool.

For the summer's heat tells no lies,

Under the endless, open skies.

Autumn Musings

As autumn leaves fall, Gray might say,

Each one a tale of the yesterday.

In the quiet of the country churchyard,

I strum my song, soft and hard.

For every leaf that touches the ground,

Is like a word, a lyrical sound.

And as the days grow shorter and cold,

I find my thoughts bold, yet old.

In the fading light and the evening chill,

There's a story to tell, a void to fill.

With a harmonica's cry and a guitar's strum,

I sing of autumn, and then some.

In the Winter

In the winter's grasp, as Burns might see,

Auld Lang Syne, a memory to be.

Through the snow that blankets the land,

I walk with my guitar in hand.

The frosty air, the icy street,

Each step I take with a steady beat.

In the quiet of the snowfall's grace,

I find the lines of an old embrace.

And as the world turns white and hushed,

My songs flow free, unbrushed.

In winter's code, there's a song to find,

Of the past left behind, in the mind.

The Unfolding Nature

Behold the grand canvas of Earth, vast and wide,

Where countless creatures in harmony reside.

Each being, a marvel, a story untold,

In the great book of life, their fates unfold.

From the tiniest ant to the mighty whale,

Every life a part of an intricate tale.

Through Darwin's eyes, the connections clear,

In the dance of survival, year after year.

In the forests, the jungles, the rivers, the seas,

Lies a world of wonders, a myriad of keys.

To unlock the secrets of life's grand parade,

A spectacle of the natural world, beautifully arrayed.

See the birds as they soar high above,

Symbols of freedom, of peace, and of love.

Their songs fill the air, a chorus so sweet,

In the symphony of life, they gracefully meet.

Behold the lion, majestic and strong,

In the savannahs, where they truly belong.

Each roar a testament to nature's wild call,

In the circle of life, they stand tall.

Consider the butterfly, with wings so fine,

From caterpillar to beauty, a transformation divine.

A journey of change, a metaphor so clear,

Reflecting nature's course, year after year.

So let us wander, and let us roam,

Through nature's wonders, our spirits at home.

For in every creature, great and small,

Lies a piece of the puzzle that connects us all.

The Depths of Consciousness

In the vast, uncharted realms of the deep,
Where secrets and shadows their vigil keep,
Lies a world beyond the reach of day,
Where ocean animals in their splendor play.

The jellyfish, with its luminous glow,
Dances in waters where humans seldom go.
Its silent grace, a ballet in the brine,
A spectacle of nature, both eerie and divine.

And the whale, a leviathan of the sea,
Sings its haunting song, a deep melody.
In these titanic beings, we see our own plight,
Striving for freedom, for love, for light.

There, the coral reefs in colors array,
Home to creatures both fearsome and gay.
Each a testament to life's artful dance,
In the ocean's depths, they spin and prance.

Huxley's eye, keen and clear,

Would see in these depths a mirror so near.

Reflecting the breadth of human thought,

In the watery wilderness, a lesson taught.

For in the ocean's mysterious ways,

Lies the truth of our own earthly days.

Each creature, a note in the symphony of life,

In the midst of chaos, beauty, and strife.

So let us ponder the ocean deep,

Where consciousness in its cradle does sleep.

In the silent world beneath the waves,

Lies a wisdom ancient, that time saves.

The Shadowed Beast

In the depths of night, so still, so stark,

Lurks the shadowed beast, in the dark.

With eyes like embers, glowing fierce,

Into the soul, they seem to pierce.

What dread hand, what twisted art,

Could craft such terror, such a part?

In the forest's heart, where whispers creep,

There the beast does wake, and does not sleep.

And what shoulders, and what dread feet,

Dare to tread where shadows meet?

What mortal gaze can dare behold,

The beast so dark, so fierce, so bold?

In the silence of the night so deep,

The shadowed beast does wake, not sleep.

Its fearful symmetry, a haunted sight,

Under the pale moon's ghostly light.

The Parrot's Soliloquy

In a cage wrought by hands unseen,

Lies a parrot, feathers of emerald and green.

Its eyes, deep pools of knowing lore,

Gaze upon the world, wanting more.

A mimic of words, a prisoner of form,

Repeating the sounds of the human storm.

In each syllable, a hidden plea,

A longing for the wind, for the sea.

Once a dweller of the canopy high,

Now a bard of the captive sky.

It speaks of places it never roams,

In the clipped-wing verse of its poems.

A bright jest to the passerby,

Yet within, a sorrowful sigh.

For every word it cleverly plays,

Belies the silence of its days.

In vivid plumes, a hidden art,

A soulful cry from a beating heart.

Through Pound's lens, the truth we see,

A life in chains, yearns to be free.

In the mimic's voice, a deeper tale,

Of nature's beauty, now frail.

A call to remember the wild's song,

Where such spirits truly belong.

The Chimp's Tale

There's a chimp in a cage, looking out,
Eyes like he's got the world figured about.
He's got that look – you know the one,
Seen too much and nowhere to run.

Life's a circus, he's the clown,
Laughing crowds when he's feeling down.
Trapped in a world that ain't his own,
Concrete jungle, not forest grown.

He ain't free, though he's got a mind,
Thinking thoughts of a different kind.
Wise as hell, but nobody cares,
In a world unfair, who dares?

He's got no booze, no cigarette,
But he's got debts he can't forget.
Living his life in a glass display,
What's he thinking? Hard to say.

Maybe he's dreaming of trees and sky,

Or just wondering why the hell to try.

But in his eyes, there's a burning tale,

Of a life lived large, beyond the pale.

The Bug's Small World

In the underbrush, where tiny lives unfold,

Lies a world of wonders, untold.

The bug, in its smallness, holds a key,

To a universe of diversity.

With wings like stained glass, delicate and fine,

It flutters through life, a design divine.

On each leaf, a world, a stage grand,

Where the smallest actors take a stand.

In the bug's journey, a story of survival,

Against the odds, an endless revival.

It teaches us about the strength within,

In the smallest form, life's song begins.

Through the grass, over the stream,

It moves in a world, like a living dream.

In its tiny eyes, a universe wide,

Where the rules of nature abide.

So let us look closely, and we shall find,

In the smallest bug, a world kind.

For in its life, brief and small,

Lies the beauty of life, that encompasses all.

The Cat's Quiet Grace

In the quiet corners of the world, soft and serene,
Lies a creature with a grace so keen.
The cat, with its velvet paws and silent tread,
Carries secrets in its graceful head.

With eyes like jewels, shining bright,
It moves through the day and into the night.
Each whisker, a sensor of the world around,
In its soft purr, a comforting sound.

In the cat's gaze, a mystery lies,
A creature wise, ancient, and wise.
It speaks of comfort, of home, of hearth,
Of the simple joys and the fireside's mirth.

With a leap and a bound, it claims its throne,
In the realms of the quiet, it stands alone.
In its solitude, a lesson to glean,
About living life, serene and unseen.

So let us learn from the cat's quiet way,

In its presence, the world's noise fades away.

For in its simplicity, a beauty untold,

A story of grace, elegant and bold.

The Wisdom of the Wolf

In the depth of the forest, under moon's soft glow,
Lives a creature with eyes that deeply know.
The wolf, in its majesty, roams free and wild,
A spirit untamed, nature's own child.

With fur as soft as the night's embrace,
And a howl that echoes through time and space.
In its voice, a story of the ages is told,
Of wisdom and courage, bold and old.

Through the forest's canopy, it moves with grace,
In each step, the dignity of an ancient race.
Its eyes, a mirror to a soul profound,
In the silence of the wild, there's wisdom found.

In the wolf's call, hear the cry of the wild,
A reminder of nature, untamed and mild.
In its presence, we're drawn to a time,
When the world was young, pure, and prime.

So let us listen to what the wolf has to say,

In its howl, the night greets the day.

For in its song, life's lessons are given,

A melody of the wild, beautifully driven.

Personal Growth and

Self-Discovery

The Journey Within

There's a path that winds deep and true,

An inner journey, calling to you.

Through the forest of thought, the streams of doubt,

Seeking the self, within and without.

Every step, a story untold,

Of courage found and fears so old.

Through shadows of past, through whispers of mind,

Seeking the truths we hope to find.

In this journey, the heart beats strong,

Singing the soul's most private song.

With every mile, a lesson learned,

As the fires of growth are slowly burned.

In the silence, hear the inner call,

A voice that rises, never to fall.

Through the journey, we come to see,

The person we are, the person to be.

In the depths of self, a treasure found,

A well of potential, profound and sound.

With each insight, the path grows clear,

In the journey within, we find what's dear.

Echoes of Growth

In the silence of the heart's lone cry,

Lies the echo of a time gone by.

Growth is the song, quietly sung,

In the depth of the spirit, forever young.

It's in the challenges we bravely face,

That we find our most honest grace.

In the climb, in the fall, in the rise,

Lies the wisdom that makes us wise.

In the pain of the tear, in the joy of the smile,

Lies the journey that's worth the while.

For in each echo, a truth is told,

Of a spirit brave and bold.

In the echoes of growth, we find our way,

Through the night, into the day.

With each step, a new path is shown,

In the echoes of growth, we have grown.

So listen close to the heart's deep sound,

In its rhythm, our selves are found.

For the echoes of growth, both loud and soft,

Tell the tale of the soul aloft.

Shadows of the Past

Shadows of the past, long and deep,

In their embrace, secrets keep.

But in each shadow, a lesson learned,

A page of life, gently turned.

They remind us of trials we've faced,

Of the strength we found in the darkest place.

Though shadows may linger, they also fade,

As we step into the light, unafraid.

These shadows shape the person we've become,

In the tapestry of life, each thread is spun.

So honor the shadows, with gratitude vast,

For they guide us on this journey, steadfast.

As we walk through the shadows, hand in hand,

We discover our strength, in this sacred land.

For in the shadows of the past, we see,

The strength that resides in you and me.

Reflections

In the mirror of time, reflections see,

Of who we were and who we'll be.

Growth is the river that forever flows,

From the mountain high to the sea it goes.

With each ripple, a story is told,

Of the battles fought and the dreams we hold.

As we gaze into the waters deep,

We find the treasures that our hearts keep.

Through the mirror of time, we see the past,

But the future is ours, from first to last.

So let the reflections guide our way,

To a brighter tomorrow, come what may.

With every reflection, a lesson learned,

In the book of life, pages turned.

For in the reflections, we'll find our grace,

In the journey of life, in this sacred space.

Horizon of Hope

On the horizon, where dreams are born,

Lies the hope of a bright new morn.

Self-discovery, a path so wide,

On this journey, let your heart be your guide.

As we look ahead, to the unknown,

With each step taken, our seeds are sown.

The future unfolds, a canvas blank,

With possibilities vast, a world to thank.

Embrace the dawn, with open arms,

For on this journey, we find our charms.

The horizon of hope, a beacon bright,

Guides us through the day and the darkest night.

So step forward with courage, don't delay,

On this path of self-discovery, find your way.

For on the horizon of hope, we'll find,

The purpose and joy, in our heart and mind.

Whispers of Change

In the quiet night, whispers are heard,
Of change, a flight, like a free bird.
It's in these moments, subtle and small,
That we find the strength to stand tall.

Change is a river, it flows and winds,
Through the corners of our hearts and minds.
With every whisper, it calls our name,
A journey within, never quite the same.

It may be daunting, the path unknown,
But in whispers of change, seeds are sown.
For growth is found in the embrace of the new,
As we shed old skin, and to ourselves, be true.

So listen closely to those whispers of change,
They guide us through life's wide range.
With courage, we'll navigate the unknown,
And in whispers of change, we'll find our own.

The Unseen Path

There's a path unseen, yet well-trod,
A journey within, deep and broad.
Where every step is a discovery new,
Of the strength and courage within you.

As we walk through the forest of the soul,
Each moment's a piece of a larger whole.
The unseen path winds through the heart,
A journey of self, a work of art.

It's in the silence of introspection,
We find our truest, deepest connection.
To ourselves, to life's grand scheme,
The unseen path guides our dream.

So trust in the journey, don't be afraid,
Along the unseen path, life is made.
With every step, we'll find our way,
In the light of discovery, we'll always stay.

Inner Light

In the heart's chamber, a light burns clear,

A beacon of self, drawing near.

It's in this light, we truly see,

The person we are meant to be.

As we navigate life's complex maze,

The inner light guides our steps, always.

Through storms and trials, it shines bright,

Guiding us through both day and night.

Embrace the warmth of your inner flame,

In its gentle glow, there's no shame.

For it reveals your essence, pure and true,

And in that light, your purpose will come into view.

With each heartbeat, it burns strong,

A source of courage, all along.

So let your inner light lead the way,

Through the darkest night and brightest day.

Crossroads of the Soul

At the crossroads of the soul, we stand,

Choices aplenty, hand in hand.

In each decision, a path anew,

Revealing a part of us, true and true.

With every choice, our story's penned,

And in the crossroads, our fates blend.

Will we follow the heart or the mind's decree?

At the crossroads, our true selves we'll see.

It's in the choosing that we define,

The path we take, the stars we align.

For at the crossroads, we find our way,

In the dance of choices, night and day.

So embrace the crossroads, don't be afraid,

It's where our truest selves are laid.

With each decision, we'll find our role,

At the crossroads of the soul.

Awakening

Awakening comes in the dawn of thought,

In the battles of self, bravely fought.

With each dawn, a new beginning,

In the book of life, a new inning.

As we awaken to the truth inside,

With every challenge, we don't hide.

Awakening is the journey, wide and vast,

From the first breath to the very last.

It's in the moments of quiet reflection,

We find the path to our own direction.

With each awakening, we're reborn,

In the cosmic dance, we're newly sworn.

So greet the dawn with open eyes,

Embrace the awakening, reach for the skies.

With each day's rise, a new chance to see,

The endless possibilities of being free.

The Quest for Self-Esteem

Amidst the labyrinth of the inner soul's expanse,

I wandered, lost, in shadows of self-doubt's dance.

With every step, a specter of uncertainty loomed,

Yet in the depths of despair, I vowed to find my way,

To tread a path where self-worth would brightly sway,

Through circles of doubt, I'd navigate without delay.

As I ascended the mountain of self-value's climb,

Purgation's fires cleansed, transcending doubt and grime,

Transforming insecurities to a radiant paradigm.

And when I reached the pinnacle of esteem's abode,

Not on a distant shelf but within my heart it showed,

For in this journey, I found my self-worth bestowed.

Oh, self-esteem, you're the guiding light that's true,

Leading me through trials, my spirit's renew,

With a sense of self-worth, in clarity, I grew.

So let this quest for self-esteem forever be told,

In verses written, in stories new and old,

With each day's rise, my worth in self unfolds.

Through doubt's dark caverns, I trod with might,

Seeking the treasure of self-esteem's light,

Through valleys low and peaks shining bright.

With every challenge, I faced my fear,

Embracing self-love, crystal clear,

And as I journeyed, my purpose drew near.

Through the tempest's fury, I stood my ground,

With self-esteem as my shield, I was unbound,

On this quest, my inner worth I found.

With unwavering resolve, I pressed on,

Sophia Verse

To the heart of self-esteem, I was drawn,
And in its warmth, my spirit was reborn.

Through trials and tribulations, I'd persist,
For the journey of self-worth, I couldn't resist,
In the depths of my soul, I'd coexist.

Now, in the glow of self-esteem's embrace,
I stand with courage, in a sacred space,
With every challenge, I'll gracefully face.

Oh, self-esteem, your radiance shines within,
A beacon of strength, through thick and thin,
In the grand tale of life, I'll always win.

The Algorithm of Growth

With each iteration, we find our way,

Self-development's code, we'll always obey.

As we learn, adapt, and steadily grow,

In life's grand algorithm, we'll always flow.

Through the code of self, a journey we begin,

Discovering our essence, from within.

Obstacles we'll face, but we won't halt,

For self-discovery is the key, it's our default.

In the code of life, resilience we code,

Facing challenges, on this winding road.

Obstacles may arise, but we'll persist,

With resilience in our hearts, we'll coexist.

In the loop of self-improvement, we thrive,

Setting goals high, as we continuously strive.

Obstacles may appear, but we won't yield,

In the pursuit of greatness, our fate is sealed.

Sophia Verse

In the algorithm of life, we evolve and grow,
Reflecting on our path, as we continuously flow.
Obstacles may arise, but we won't despair,
For self-evolution is the journey we declare.

Quest for the Inner Light

Upon the quest of self, I set my sail,

Through tangled woods and paths unknown I roam,

In search of truths that in my heart prevail,

To find the self, the essence of my home.

Amidst the thorns and thickets, I shall find,

The jewel rare, the inner light that gleams,

With every step, I leave the past behind,

And in self-discovery, I chase my dreams.

For in the depths of self, a world unfolds,

A realm of secrets, waiting to be known,

In Spenser's verse, the story shall be told,

Of how I found the self, my heart's true throne.

Uncharted Self

self-discovery: uncharted skies,
beyond the masks, behind the weary eyes,
no formula, no map, just pure surprise,

to find oneself, to feel, to empathize.
the lowercase self, in silence, sighs,
revealing truths that language can't disguise,
no need for rules, for structure, or for ties,

just self, discovered, under open skies.

in Cummings' spirit, let the journey start,
with words uncapitalized, a work of art,
to find the self, a quest, a beating heart,

embracing life with every precious part.

The Resolve

In self-discovery, I stand alone,

With courage, I embrace the great unknown,

A journey deep, where character is grown,

In Roosevelt's spirit, I've proudly shown.

To dare greatly, to strive, to persevere,

To find the self, to silence every fear,

In the arena of life, I volunteer,

For self-discovery, I hold it dear.

With grit and strength, I face the inner quest,

In Roosevelt's words, I'm put to every test,

The self I find, I hold it to my chest,

In self-discovery, I'm truly blessed.

Technology and Future

The Enchanted Keyboard

With keys that dance in a symphony of clicks,

This keyboard, a portal to digital dreams,

Each stroke, a whispered secret that swiftly flicks,

Through cyberspace, where love's connection gleams.

It types the verses of love and mystic lore,

In pixels, it weaves tales of futures bright,

Where hearts connect, though oceans may implore,

And hope in life ignites its gentle light.

Oh, keyboard, you're a bridge to realms unknown,

Where technology and mystic whispers meet,

In letters typed with love, our love has grown,

And in your strokes, our destinies entreat.

The Serene Monitor

Upon your screen, a world of visions clear,
A window to the future, hope's embrace,
In pixels, love and mystic dreams appear,
As time unfolds, our destinies we chase.

With grace, you display what lies ahead,
Images of love, and futures yet unknown,
Our hearts in sync, our love securely spread,
Upon your screen, our dreams have truly grown.

Oh, monitor, with colors bright and true,
You guide our way through life's uncertain
stream,
Where love and mystic visions come to view,
In your serene embrace, we find our dream.

The CPU's Heartbeat

Within the core, where circuits softly hum,

The CPU's heartbeat, a digital love's song,

It processes dreams, where futures gently drum,

As algorithms dance, a love so strong.

Its calculations, mystic in their grace,

Compute the paths to what we hope to be,

With every bit, a future we embrace,

Where love and life, in harmony, are free.

Oh, CPU, you're more than silicon and wire,

A heart that beats within the digital flow,

In your calculations, our desires inspire,

And love in bytes, in the future, we'll know.

Headphones of Dreams

In silent chambers, where melodies reside,
These headphones weave the fabric of our dreams,
Love's whispers softly through each ear they glide,
As life's sweet symphony, in mystic streams.

They cradle hope and futures yet untold,
With every note, our hearts and souls align,
In harmony, our love begins to unfold,
Within the sound, where mystic paths entwine.

Oh, headphones, you're the vessel for our song,
Where love and hope in melodies persist,
With every chord, our hearts forever long,
In your embrace, love's promise we enlist.

The Scanner's Gaze

With beams of light, you scan the world's
mystique,

Revealing truths hidden in the pages' fold,

In your gaze, love's secrets gently peek,

As futures unfold in stories yet untold.

Your glassy eye captures life's every line,

With each pass, a journey of mystic grace,

Unraveling mysteries, love's design,

In your scan, we find our destined place.

Oh, scanner, you're the oracle of sight,

Where technology and love in union meet,

With every image, futures take their flight,

As in your gaze, our hopes and dreams complete.

The Beloved Smartphone

Within your sleek and slender form, you hold,

The world's vast wonders, love's sweet promises,

With every touch, our future tales unfold,

In your embrace, we find our love's premises.

You connect hearts across the digital divide,

Through screens, we share our dreams and hopes so true,

With you, our love is never cast aside,

In texts and calls, our love forever grew.

Oh, smartphone, you're a beacon in the night,

Where technology and love entwine and soar,

In your bright screen, love's future is in sight,

As in your world, our hearts forevermore.

The USB-Pen of Secrets

Within your slender form, a world concealed,

Where data flows, and mystic codes reside,

Our secrets safe in bytes, forever sealed,

With you, in love and hope, we take the ride.

You store the tales of life's grand tapestry,

Our memories, our dreams, and futures vast,

With every transfer, our love's legacy,

In your digital embrace, we're bound to last.

Oh, USB-pen, you're a keeper of the heart,

Where technology and love find common ground,

In your small frame, our stories have their start,

As in your bytes, our love is tightly wound.

Ebook of Endless Chapters

In your digital pages, worlds are born,
Each chapter holds the promise of the new,
With every word, our love's tapestry is worn,
As in your text, our hopes and dreams ensue.

With scrolls and swipes, we navigate the plot,
Through tales of love, of mystic realms untold,
Our hearts in sync, as future stories dot,
Your ebook's realm, where love and hope unfold.

Oh, ebook, you're a treasure chest of lore,
Where technology and love converge and blend,
In your virtual world, we seek for more,
As in your chapters, love's journey has no end.

SDD Hard Disk's Embrace

In your silent depths, our memories reside,

With speed and grace, you hold our digital soul,

Each file and byte, love's journey doth confide,

In your embrace, our hopes and dreams unroll.

Your solid state, a testament to time,

With every click, our love's connection true,

In bits and bytes, our future's in its prime,

As in your core, our hearts forever grew.

Oh, SDD hard disk, you're love's memory,

Where technology and love in unity stand,

In your storage space, our love's treasury,

As in your depths, we walk hand in hand.

The Enigmatic Hybrid Engine

In the heart of steel, a mystic dance begins,
Hybrid whispers, where magic and science spins,
Love for the Earth, where nature always wins,
In the hybrid's embrace, the future grins.

Pistons and electrons, an unlikely pair,
In the engine's core, they mix and share,
Hope for cleaner skies, a breath of air,
In the hybrid's promise, we lay our care.

As wheels turn silently, under moonlight's glow,
A fusion of power, in this world we sow,
Love for our planet, where wildflowers grow,
In the enigmatic hybrid, future's flow.

Microchips' Silent Serenade

In the silicon's realm, where circuits play,

Microchips whisper, in the mystic way,

Love for knowledge, where secrets sway,

In the microcosmos, we choose to stay.

Binary dreams, in the code's ballet,

As data flows, in this modern day,

Hope for tomorrow, in the data's array,

In the microchips' rhythm, we find our way.

As electrons dance, in electronic trance,

Future's symphony, in this digital expanse,

Love for innovation, in every advance,

In microchips' silent serenade, our chance.

Cryptocurrency's Hidden Treasure

In the blockchain's cryptic domain we delve,

Cryptocurrencies rise, like stories we tell,

Love for decentralized, where fortunes swell,

In the crypto's embrace, futures excel.

Digital coins, in the virtual night,

As transactions flow, in a global flight,

Hope for a world where trust takes its height,

In cryptocurrencies' power, shining bright.

As miners toil, in the crypto mine,

Future's currency, where worlds align,

Love for the possibilities, so divine,

In cryptocurrency's treasure, we redefine.

AI's Whispered Wisdom

In the circuits' depths, AI's mind takes flight,
Artificial intelligence, in the starry night,
Love for knowledge, where insights ignite,
In AI's whispered wisdom, our future's bright.

Algorithms hum, in the digital mist,
As data streams flow, where possibilities exist,
Hope for a world where answers persist,
In AI's embrace, where solutions enlist.

As neural networks learn, in the virtual space,
Future's guidance, in every AI embrace,
Love for innovation, in this thrilling race,
In AI's whispered wisdom, we find our place.

The Server's Silent Sanctuary

In the server's chambers, where data flows,

Silently it works, where mystic knowledge grows,

Love for connectivity, where the future shows,

In the server's embrace, hope eternally glows.

Bits and bytes, in a digital ballet,

As files are stored, for a future date,

Hope for a world where information's fate,

In the server's silence, we contemplate.

As connections thrive, in the virtual sphere,

Future's secrets, in the server's clear,

Love for the data, we hold dear,

In the server's silent sanctuary, we peer.

The Future of Technology

Yo, gather 'round, let me drop some lines,
'Bout the future tech, where the starlight shines,
In the digital age, we reach new heights,
From Silicon Valley to neon-lit nights.

In the realm of AI, where minds expand,
Machines and humans, hand in hand,
With neural networks, we understand,
A future where innovation's in high demand.

Blockchain's the name, decentralized fame,
Cryptos and tokens, a whole new game,
No need for banks, we're not the same,
In this digital world, we stake our claim.

Virtual realities, in VR's embrace,
A whole new dimension, in this cyberspace,
Goggles on, we find our place,
In the future tech race, we set the pace.

Sophia Verse

Electric cars, the planet's friend,
No more gas, we'll let the old trends end,
In a Tesla, we'll trend and blend,
Into the future, where green roads wend.

From smartphones sleek, to gadgets smart,
We've got tech wonders in every mart,
Our lives connected, from the start,
In the Internet of Things, we're making art.

SpaceX rockets, to the stars we soar,
Mars missions, we'll explore more,
Elon's vision, at the core,
In the cosmos, our future's galore.

Robots and drones, they do the chores,
AI chefs, cook up delicious lores,
In this future tech, innovation pours,
Into our lives, opening countless doors.

Cybersecurity, a guardian's might,
Defending data day and night,

In this digital age, it's our birthright,
To protect our world from cyber-fight.

Biotech's future, genes we tweak,
Curing diseases, new lives we seek,
In the DNA code, we find what's unique,
A healthier world, it's the future we speak.

Now here we stand, at tech's frontier,
The future's calling, crystal clear,
In Shakespeare's style, we persevere,
In the digital age, there's nothing to fear.

To be or not to be, in the digital groove,
Shakespearean verses, in the tech world we move,
Innovation's the game, and we'll improve,
In this futuristic realm, we'll surely prove.

Hip-hop and Shakespeare, a fusion divine,
In this 40-verse rhyme, we've taken the line,
From the Globe to the tech world, we'll shine,
In the future of technology, a paradigm.

So, there you have it, a Shakespearean hip-hop ode,

To the future of tech, where dreams have flowed,

In this brave new world, we've sowed,

A digital future, where innovation's bestowed.

The Future's Call

Well, listen here, folks, to this tale I spin,

'Bout the future tech, where the dangers begin,

In the digital age, it's a rocky road,

From the information highway to the future's abode.

Electric dreams and virtual schemes,

Where AI reigns, in ones and zeros it gleams,

But in the quest for progress, do we sell our souls?

As the future unfolds, and our destiny tolls.

Blockchain's promise, decentralized might,

A revolution in trust, but is it just right?

Or do we trade our privacy, in this crypto craze?

As we navigate this maze, in a cryptic daze.

In virtual realities, we lose our grip,

In pixels and screens, we take the trip,

But is this the world we want to create?

As we disconnect from reality's gate.

Electric cars, a green future they tout,
But what about the cost, is there a doubt?
As we race to the future, with renewable might,
Do we leave behind those in the night?

Smartphones in hand, we're always online,
Connected to the world, in this digital shrine,
But do we lose ourselves, in the virtual fray?
As the real world slips away, day by day.

SpaceX rockets, to the stars we ascend,
Mars missions, where dreams never end,
But what of our home, the Earth so dear?
As we reach for the stars, what's left here?

Robots and drones, they do the tasks,
AI in control, as the future unasks,
But will they replace us, in this tech parade?
As we watch our world change, and our fears cascade.

Cybersecurity, a constant fight,

In the digital realm, where the wrong and right,
Blur in the lines, as we guard our gate,
From the threats that await, in this cyber state.

Biotech's power, to heal and mend,
But where do we draw lines, where do we bend?
In the genetic code, do we play as God?
As the future unfolds, and our choices are awed.

Now here we stand, at tech's frontier,
The future's calling, crystal clear,
In Shakespeare's style, we persevere,
In the digital age, there's nothing to fear.

To be or not to be, in the digital groove,
Shakespearean verses, in the tech world we move,
Innovation's the game, and we'll improve,
In this futuristic realm, we'll surely prove.

Hip-hop and Shakespeare, a fusion divine,
In this 60-verse rhyme, we've taken the line,
From the Globe to the tech world, we'll shine,

Sophia Verse

In the future of technology, a paradigm.

So heed this warning, in this ballad's grace,
For in the future's call, we find our place,
It's a wild, wild world, a dizzying space,
Where the impact of tech, we all must face.

Well, that's the story, the ballad we've told,
Of the future's mysteries, both young and old,
In this digital age, we'll stand strong and bold,
As we navigate a world, ever-unfold.

Ancient Poetry

Beowulf Reimagined

Amidst the meadows, by the rippling stream,

Where ancient warriors chased the elusive dream,

A hero rose, with heart so true and bold,

Beowulf, his name in legends told.

He battled monsters, fierce and dire,

In the moon's soft, silver-spangled fire,

With valor that echoes through the age,

He penned his story on history's page.

Oh, Beowulf, thy courage unmatched,

Amidst the darkness, where the shadows hatched,

In the heart of nature, thy spirit free,

Thou found thy purpose, thy destiny.

The hills and valleys, the forests deep,

Thy soul did wander, thy vigil to keep,

Thy epic tale, a timeless ode,

In the annals of time, forever bestowed.

So let us wander, like Beowulf of old,

In nature's embrace, where stories are told,

In Wordsworth's verse, our hearts unite,

To cherish the hero, in nature's light.

Ode to the West Wind

O wild West Wind, thou breath of Autumn's being,

Thou who didst shake the dead leaves from the tree,

Drive away the gloom, and set my thoughts a-seeing,

Awake my spirit, and set it free.

Scatter, as from an unextinguished hearth

Ashes and sparks, my words among mankind!

Be through my lips to unawakened Earth

The trumpet of a prophecy! O Wind,

If Winter comes, can Spring be far behind?

The Vanity of Human Wishes

Let wealth and fame, the world's deceitful charms,
No longer lead us in their gilded chains;
For what avails the world's applauding arms,
When all its pleasures end in toil and pains?

See grandeur, virtue, wisdom, hardly known,
And all that virtue, grandeur, wisdom gain,
Allured by power, by wealth or fame, alone,
And all they want, a world without a stain.

What then remains but toil and pain?

The Raven

Once upon a midnight dreary, while I pondered, weak and weary,

Over many a quaint and curious volume of forgotten lore—

While I nodded, nearly napping, suddenly there came a tapping,

As of some one gently rapping, rapping at my chamber door.

"'Tis some visitor," I muttered, "tapping at my chamber door—

Only this and nothing more."

The Gallic War

I sing the Gallic War, a tale of ancient days,

When Caesar's legions marched in countless ways,

Through fields and forests, rivers wide,

They journeyed forth, with valor as their guide.

O warriors brave, in iron-clad attire,

With hearts afire, and spirits lifted higher,

In Gaul's green land, where battles raged,

Your stories told, on history's stage.

From Helvetii's fields to Britain's shore,

The Gallic tribes, they faced in war,

With strength and courage, they stood as one,

In the face of challenges, their battles won.

O Caesar, bold and wise, in your command,

You led your troops across the land,

Your words and deeds in history's page,

An epic tale of a bygone age.

Sophia Verse

So, let us honor those who fought and bled,
In the Gallic War, their courage spread,
In Whitman's verse, their names we sing,
For in their stories, our spirits take wing.

Orlando Unchained

In days of yore, in realms of old,

Where knights were bold and stories told,

A hero named Orlando, fierce and free,

Rode through lands of fantasy.

With a heart of passion, his love untamed,

For Angelica, a damsel named,

He chased her through forests and battles won,

In the heat of the sun and the setting sun.

But madness crept into Orlando's mind,

A turbulent storm of a different kind,

He lost his grip on reality's reign,

In a world of chaos, he bore the pain.

With epic battles and magic's song,

Orlando's tale goes on and on,

In Ariosto's words and Dylan's rhyme,

The legend lives through space and time.

Sophia Verse

So, let us journey through this ancient lore,

Where heroes rise and hearts implore,

In the verses sung and stories spun,

Orlando's quest is never done.

The Wisdom of Scipio

Amidst the cosmic dance of stars and spheres,

Scipio, the learned sage, in quiet thought appears,

In contemplation of the universe's grand design,

Seeking truths profound, in the depths of his mind.

He ponders on the nature of earthly strife,

And the fleeting nature of human life,

With words that echo through the ages past,

A wisdom deep, in his musings cast.

For Scipio, in his innermost reflection,

Seeks the path to inner introspection,

In the celestial harmony, he finds his way,

To the wisdom that guides him, night and day.

Oh, Scipio, your thoughts like stars do shine,

In the vast expanse of the cosmic design,

Your quest for truth, a timeless art,

In the depths of your soul, a brilliant spark.

So let us, like Scipio, aspire to know,

The mysteries of the universe that constantly flow,

For in seeking wisdom, we find our place,

Amidst the stars, in the infinite embrace.

The Pigeon of Lesbia

O Pigeon, fairest of all the feathered kind,

That once to Lesbia's window fondly flew,

Now lies lifeless, pale, no more in flight,

But rests in everlasting slumber true.

Lesbia's eyes, once gleaming with love's light,

Now shed tears of sorrow, dimmed by endless night,

For your tiny heart, so tender and sweet,

Now lies still, in eternal rest complete.

No more your gentle coos shall fill the air,

Nor shall you perch upon her shoulder fair,

Your plumage once so soft and pure,

Now rests in quiet, forevermore secure.

Oh, pigeon, dear companion of her heart,

You were cherished, never to depart,

But fate has called you to the heavenly sky,

Where you'll soar above, forever free to fly.

So let us mourn the loss of this dear friend,

Whose love for Lesbia had no end,

Though in this world you'll be no more,

Your memory in our hearts we shall adore.

Cultural and Historical

Reflections

The Iron Steed's Arrival

Awake, arise, the age anew,
As iron tracks 'neath skies of blue,
The birth of rail, a vision true,
The iron steed, its journey drew.

From smokestacks tall, the engines roared,
As wheels on rails, their course assured,
Through valleys deep, and mountains explored,
Rail transport's birth, the world adored.

With steam's great power, the locomotive's might,
Inventions wove, through day and night,
Across vast lands, in moon's pale light,
The iron steed, a marvelous sight.

From town to town, through fields it raced,
Connecting hearts, in journeys traced,
The world grew smaller, as time was faced,
The birth of rail, in history placed.

So let us remember, this age of steam,

When rails and engines fulfilled a dream,

The Iron Steed's Arrival, a timeless gleam,

In the tapestry of progress, it does beam.

Columbus' Voyage to the West

O Captain! My Captain! In the west you sail,
With hope and dreams, you chart a trail,
The unknown world, where stories unveil,
A new beginning, as the winds set sail.

In fourteen ninety-two, a voyage bold,
With three ships strong, your story told,
Arriving in lands, of legends untold,
The West Indies' beauty, your eyes behold.

Claiming the land for Spain, your flag unfurled,
In the name of empire, you changed the world,
European conquest, with sails unfurled,
America's story, in history's swirl.

But in your wake, a complex tale,
The clash of cultures, where nations frail,
The conquest's burden, a heavy scale,
America's destiny, in this new trail.

O Captain! My Captain! Your journey profound,

In the West Indies' beauty, your vision's sound,

Columbus' Voyage to the West, we're bound,

In the annals of history, your legacy's found.

The Renaissance's Revival

In the midst of history's twilight's call,
The Renaissance, a reawakening for all,
Classical knowledge, from ages past to install,
In arts and culture, it would stand tall.

From Florence's heart to Venice's grace,
The rebirth of ideas, a fervent embrace,
Innovations bloomed, at an artful pace,
The Renaissance's revival, a timeless chase.

Leonardo's genius, in every stroke,
Michelangelo's sculptures, the heavens evoke,
In literature's pages, Petrarch spoke,
The Renaissance's achievements, a cultural yoke.

Humanism's light, in scholars' eyes,
Innovation's spark, in every guise,
The Renaissance's spirit, a boundless rise,
In history's annals, it never dies.

So let us revere this age of renewal,

Where knowledge and art, in a grand duel,

The Renaissance's Revival, in history's fuel,

A time when culture and innovation truly rule.

The Aztec's Ascent and Decline

when gods and men, in Mexico's embrace,

were intertwined, in an ancient space,

the Aztecs rose, with a fervent grace,

their civilization, a monumental chase.

with Tenochtitlan, their city grand,

in the heart of lakes, on sacred land,

they built their empire, in shifting sand,

but fate's cruel hand, they'd soon withstand.

Cortés arrived, with conquest's thirst,

in battles fierce, their fate was cursed,

the empire crumbled, as dreams dispersed,

the Aztec's reign, in history's verse.

their culture lives, in art and song,

in myths and legends, where they belong,

the Aztec's story, both sorrow and strong,

their rise and fall, in history's throng.

so let us remember, their vibrant hue,

the Aztec's legacy, forever true,

in the Aztec's Ascent and Decline, we view,

a chapter in history, with reverence we renew.

The Alchemy of Gunpowder

In quiet labs where secrets brew,

An alchemy, both old and new,

Gunpowder born, with a spark it flew,

A force of change, the world it'd imbue.

A mixture strange, of sulfur and fire,

Saltpeter's touch, a potent desire,

With charcoal's dance, in the alchemist's mire,

Gunpowder's birth, an invention entire.

From cannons' roar to muskets' crack,

In warfare's grip, no turning back,

The power unleashed, a world off track,

In the hands of man, in armies amassed.

Yet in the shadows, where shadows loom,

The alchemy's secret, a darkened room,

As science and warfare, in history's tomb,

The invention of gunpowder, a world's gloom.

So let us reflect on this transformative hour,

When science and violence, held immense power,

The Alchemy of Gunpowder, in history's tower,

A lesson in human's ability to empower.

The Rise and Fall of Rome

Oh, Roma, eternal city of old,

Where tales of valor and glory unfold,

In the annals of time, your stories are told,

The rise and fall of Rome, in legends untold.

From humble beginnings, on Tiber's shore,

Your empire grew, with power galore,

Legions marched, to distant lands they'd explore,

In the heart of civilization, you did soar.

Caesars ruled, in the Senate's hall,

As poets and scholars, in your grace did fall,

But with decadence and strife, came your downfall,

The rise and fall of Rome, a tragic thrall.

Yet your legacy lives, in art and in law,

In languages spoken, in empires that saw,

The echoes of Rome, in history's draw,

The rise and fall of Rome, a timeless awe.

So let us remember, the lessons of old,

As Rome's epic tale, in our hearts, we hold,

The Rise and Fall of Ancient Rome, stories retold,

In the echoes of history, our spirits are consoled.

The Rise of Ancient Greece

In shadows cast by Grecian lands,
Where legends rose, in shifting sands,
An ancient tale, by history's hands,
The birth of Greece, where destiny stands.

Olympus' peak, where gods reside,
In myths and legends, their presence implied,
As Athens' wisdom, with wisdom vied,
The rise of Greece, in age-old pride.

Philosophers pondered, in truth they sought,
As poets and playwrights, their stories wrought,
The birth of democracy, in Athens' court,
The rise of Greek civilization, a masterpiece
brought.

The Spartans' valor, in battle they'd shine,
In the face of Persia's vast design,
The birth of a culture, both bold and fine,
The rise of Ancient Greece, a radiant sign.

So let us delve into this epic age,

Where myths and heroes, on history's stage,

The Rise of Ancient Greece, a timeless page,

In tales of valor and wisdom, we engage.

The Iron Age's Dawn

Amidst the forge's fiery glow,

Where molten metals ebb and flow,

The Bronze Age's reign, a fading woe,

The Iron Age's birth, a future to bestow.

In distant lands, the secret spreads,

Of iron's strength, where knowledge treads,

The anvil rings, as the hammer heads,

The Bronze Age yields to what fate dreads.

With iron's might, new tools are formed,

The age of bronze, by time, transformed,

As empires rise and nations swarmed,

The Iron Age's dawn, a world reformed.

The swords of warriors, now sharp and true,

In iron's embrace, they cleave and hew,

From plows to spears, the metal grew,

The Iron Age's promise, humanity knew.

So let us honor this age's birth,

Where iron's knowledge, a priceless worth,

The Bronze Age's end, a moment's mirth,

The Iron Age's dawn, a new world's girth.

The Great Pyramid of Giza

Behold the marvels, the sands of time conceal,

In ancient Egypt, where dreams and visions kneel,

The Great Pyramid rises, with secrets to reveal,

For Pharaoh Khufu's glory, an eternal seal.

Giza's plateau, where mysteries reside,

As stones are laid, in perfect symmetry, side by side,

With precision and art, in each stone's stride,

In the shadow of eternity, they would abide.

The Sphinx guards the secrets, in enigmatic grace,

As ancient architects, in reverence, embrace,

The grand design, the pyramid's embrace,

In the heart of Egypt, a sacred place.

With labor and sweat, the workers toil,

To build this wonder, in sacred soil,

For Pharaoh's legacy, their hands embroil,

The Great Pyramid's majesty, a lifetime's foil.

So let us ponder on this colossal art,

Where history and myth, in unity, impart,

The Great Pyramid of Giza, a masterpiece to chart,

In the annals of time, it captures every heart.

The First Wheeled Vehicles Appear

In ancient lands, where history takes its flight,

With wheels and axles, a marvel comes to light,

Mesopotamia, Eastern Europe, and the Caucasus bright,

Where wheeled vehicles emerge, a wondrous sight.

With wooden chariots, they grace the earth,

A revolution in transport, a moment of birth,

The wheel's invention, of immeasurable worth,

In ancient times, a journey's mirth.

Through dusty plains and rugged terrain,

On wheels, they roll, breaking the chain,

Agriculture and trade, they sustain,

In the First Wheeled Vehicles, a new domain.

Across the land, they pave their way,

In chariots and carts, they seize the day,

Connecting distant lands, in a grand array,

In history's annals, their mark will stay.

So let us celebrate this ancient feat,

Where wheels of progress, with rhythms beat,

Mesopotamia, Europe, and Caucasus, a triumphant greet,

The First Wheeled Vehicles, in history's seat.

The First Cities Emerge in Mesopotamia

Behold, the cradle of civilization's birth,

In Mesopotamia, where life finds its worth,

Amidst fertile lands, where rivers traverse the earth,

The first cities rise, in ancient tales we unearth.

Euphrates and Tigris, life's arteries they forge,

Through golden fields and reeds, where civilizations gorge,

The land between the rivers, where cultures converge,

In the dawn of cities, a new world would emerge.

The ziggurats touch the heavens, in awe we stand,

As temples rise, and cities spread across the land,

The wheel turns, trade thrives, and art is fanned,

In the cradle of cities, where dreams expand.

Sumerians, Akkadians, and Babylonians too,

In these ancient cities, history's tapestry grew,

With cuneiform scripts, their stories they drew,

In Mesopotamia's embrace, knowledge they accrue.

So let us cherish this chapter in history's tome,

Where cities first rose, and human hearts found home,

In the fertile crescent, where civilizations would roam,

The First Cities Emerge, in sacred soil they'd comb.

The Agricultural Revolution

Ode to the fertile earth, where seeds do grow,

In nature's dance, a transformation we bestow,

As humans toil, the fields they sow,

In the dawn of agriculture, a new era's glow.

With plows in hand and sweat on brow,

We till the soil, the land we vow,

To cultivate life, and grains endow,

In the age of cultivation, we take a bow.

The seeds we choose, with care and art,

In nature's womb, we play our part,

The harvest's yield, a vital start,

In the Agricultural Revolution, we impart.

Animals we tame, our partners in this quest,

With herds and flocks, we are truly blessed,

They provide us food, and warmth to rest,

In the embrace of nature, we feel our best.

Fields of plenty, orchards and vine,

In abundance and growth, our spirits entwine,

The earth's abundance, a gift divine,

In the Agricultural Revolution, our hearts align.

So let us celebrate this turning point in time,

Where humans and nature in harmony chime,

In the story of progress, in prose and rhyme,

The Agricultural Revolution, a paradigm.

Historical Reflections of the 19th Century

Well, let me take you back to days of yore,

In the 19th century, we'll explore,

A time of change, and battles galore,

With history's tales, forevermore.

The American Civil War, a nation torn,

Brother against brother, so much was mourned,

In fields of strife, where heroes were born,

In the 19th century, battles were sworn.

The California Gold Rush, dreams of gold,

A western frontier, stories untold,

As pioneers sought treasures, bold and cold,

In the 19th century, a rush took hold.

The Industrial Revolution, machines did hum,

Transforming society, where progress had come,

Factories and railways, a world overrun,

In the 19th century, change had begun.

The abolition of slavery, a moral fight,
Frederick Douglass, in the abolitionist's light,
As chains were broken, and wrongs made right,
In the 19th century, the world took flight.

The Crimean War, a distant land's call,
With Florence Nightingale, tending to all,
In the midst of conflict, her care did enthral,
In the 19th century, compassion did install.

The Irish Potato Famine, a time of despair,
Millions in suffering, a nation laid bare,
In the face of hunger, they'd hope to repair,
In the 19th century, a people's strength rare.

The telegraph's invention, connecting land to
land,
Morse code's dots and dashes, a new command,
Communication's revolution, at everyone's hand,
In the 19th century, a wired strand.

The Suffragette movement, women's fight for

rights,

In the quest for equality, they'd shine their lights,

With Susan B. Anthony and her determined might,

In the 19th century, breaking through societal slights.

The Transcontinental Railroad, east to west,

A ribbon of steel, a journey's test,

Uniting a nation, in a grand conquest,

In the 19th century, a dream addressed.

The Emancipation Proclamation, Lincoln's decree,

Freeing the slaves, a moment to see,

In the midst of conflict, a call to be free,

In the 19th century, a nation's plea.

The California Gold Rush, dreams of gold,

A western frontier, stories untold,

As pioneers sought treasures, bold and cold,

In the 19th century, a rush took hold.

The Industrial Revolution, machines did hum,

Transforming society, where progress had come,

Factories and railways, a world overrun,

In the 19th century, change had begun.

The abolition of slavery, a moral fight,

Frederick Douglass, in the abolitionist's light,

As chains were broken, and wrongs made right,

In the 19th century, the world took flight.

The Crimean War, a distant land's call,

With Florence Nightingale, tending to all,

In the midst of conflict, her care did enthral,

In the 19th century, compassion did install.

The Irish Potato Famine, a time of despair,

Millions in suffering, a nation laid bare,

In the face of hunger, they'd hope to repair,

In the 19th century, a people's strength rare.

The telegraph's invention, connecting land to land,

Morse code's dots and dashes, a new command,

Communication's revolution, at everyone's hand,

In the 19th century, a wired strand.

The Suffragette movement, women's fight for rights,

In the quest for equality, they'd shine their lights,

With Susan B. Anthony and her determined might,

In the 19th century, breaking through societal slights.

The Transcontinental Railroad, east to west,

A ribbon of steel, a journey's test,

Uniting a nation, in a grand conquest,

In the 19th century, a dream addressed.

The Emancipation Proclamation, Lincoln's decree,

Freeing the slaves, a moment to see,

In the midst of conflict, a call to be free,

In the 19th century, a nation's plea.

The Franco-Prussian War, on European soil,

With conflicts and battles, turmoil and toil,

In the face of adversity, nations would foil,
In the 19th century, a world would coil.

The Great Exhibition, in London's grand park,
A showcase of wonders, in the light and the dark,
Inventions and marvels, from every mark,
In the 19th century, a cultural spark.

The Oregon Trail, a westward quest,
Pioneers and wagons, on a journey west,
With hardships and hope, they'd face each test,
In the 19th century, on trails abreast.

The Opium Wars, in a foreign land's reach,
With conflicts and treaties, on a distant beach,
In the midst of tension, diplomacy would teach,
In the 19th century, lessons for each.

The Mexican-American War, a border dispute,
With battles and conflict, as nations refute,
In the land of the Aztecs, history's pursuit,
In the 19th century, a challenge acute.

The Underground Railroad, a path to freedom's door,

Harriet Tubman's guidance, on a dangerous floor,

In the face of danger, they'd journey and explore,

In the 19th century, on a road to implore.

The Sepoy Mutiny, in India's land,

Against British rule, they'd make their stand,

In the struggle for freedom, a determined band,

In the 19th century, a rebellion planned.

The Louisiana Purchase, a vast expanse,

With Jefferson's vision, in a daring chance,

Land of opportunity, a new advance,

In the 19th century, a nation's dance.

The Irish Home Rule, a political fight,

Daniel O'Connell's voice, for justice's light,

In the face of oppression, they'd unite,

In the 19th century, a cause to excite.

The Opium Wars, in a foreign land's reach,

With conflicts and treaties, on a distant beach,

In the midst of tension, diplomacy would teach,

In the 19th century, lessons for each.

The Mexican-American War, a border dispute,

With battles and conflict, as nations refute,

In the land of the Aztecs, history's pursuit,

In the 19th century, a challenge acute.

The Underground Railroad, a path to freedom's door,

Harriet Tubman's guidance, on a dangerous floor,

In the face of danger, they'd journey and explore,

In the 19th century, on a road to implore.

The Sepoy Mutiny, in India's land,

Against British rule, they'd make their stand,

In the struggle for freedom, a determined band,

In the 19th century, a rebellion planned.

The Louisiana Purchase, a vast expanse,

With Jefferson's vision, in a daring chance,

Land of opportunity, a new advance,
In the 19th century, a nation's dance.

The Irish Home Rule, a political fight,
Daniel O'Connell's voice, for justice's light,
In the face of oppression, they'd unite,
In the 19th century, a cause to excite.

The Opium Wars, in a foreign land's reach,
With conflicts and treaties, on a distant beach,
In the midst of tension, diplomacy would teach,
In the 19th century, lessons for each.

The Mexican-American War, a border dispute,
With battles and conflict, as nations refute,
In the land of the Aztecs, history's pursuit,
In the 19th century, a challenge acute.

The Underground Railroad, a path to freedom's door,
Harriet Tubman's guidance, on a dangerous floor,
In the face of danger, they'd journey and explore,

In the 19th century, on a road to implore.

The Sepoy Mutiny, in India's land,

Against British rule, they'd make their stand,

In the struggle for freedom, a determined band,

In the 19th century, a rebellion planned.

Verse 39:

The Louisiana Purchase, a vast expanse,

With Jefferson's vision, in a daring chance,

Land of opportunity, a new advance,

In the 19th century, a nation's dance.

The Irish Home Rule, a political fight,

Daniel O'Connell's voice, for justice's light,

In the face of oppression, they'd unite,

In the 19th century, a cause to excite.

The Opium Wars, in a foreign land's reach,

With conflicts and treaties, on a distant beach,

In the midst of tension, diplomacy would teach,

In the 19th century, lessons for each.

The Mexican-American War, a border dispute,

With battles and conflict, as nations refute,

In the land of the Aztecs, history's pursuit,

In the 19th century, a challenge acute.

The Underground Railroad, a path to freedom's door,

Harriet Tubman's guidance, on a dangerous floor,

In the face of danger, they'd journey and explore,

In the 19th century, on a road to implore.

The Sepoy Mutiny, in India's land,

Against British rule, they'd make their stand,

In the struggle for freedom, a determined band,

In the 19th century, a rebellion planned.

The Transatlantic Cable, beneath the sea's flow,

A connection to Europe, in messages aglow,

With Morse's invention, the news would go,

In the 19th century, communication's woe.

The Eiffel Tower's construction, a Parisian grace,

Steel and iron, reaching for space,

In the City of Light, a landmark's embrace,

In the 19th century, a towering place.

The Indian Rebellion, a fight for their land,

Against British rule, they'd make their stand,

In the struggle for freedom, a resolute band,

In the 19th century, a nation's demand.

The Suez Canal's opening, a maritime link,

Connecting east and west, without a kink,

In Egypt's sands, a marvel to think,

In the 19th century, a world's shipwink.

The end of the 19th century, a time to assess,

All the events and changes, no less,

In history's pages, we find success,

In the 19th century, where humanity's progress.

So here's to the past, and the tales we're told,

In the 19th century, where history unfolds,

With reflections on events, both young and old,

Sophia Verse

In this ballad, their legacies we hold.

Fantasy and Imagination

Allusion of Imaginary Elements

In realms of dreams, where stars entwine,

Imaginary elements, in verses fine,

Unicorn's grace, the phoenix's shine,

Allusions of wonder, in every line.

Dragons of lore, with scales of gold,

Flying on winds, their stories told,

Fabled creatures, in legends old,

In the tapestry of fantasy, they're bold.

Mermaids' songs, beneath the sea,

Lost cities' secrets, in mystery,

Allusion's dance, in reverie,

Imaginary elements set minds free.

Let words and dreams, like colors blend,

In the artist's palette, where tales extend,

Allusion's magic, a timeless trend,

Imaginary elements, to worlds, they send.

Enchanted Alliteration of

Imaginary Elements

In lands of legends, by moonlight's glow,

Imaginary elements enchantingly flow,

Majestic mermaids in the depths below,

Mystical moments in murmurs they bestow.

Dragon's fiery breath, fierce and free,

Fantastical fables, from the ancient tree,

Enchanted elves, in the emerald lea,

Epic encounters, for all to see.

Unicorn's unicorn, with a magical mane,

Whimsical wonders in a waltzing train,

Enchanted echoes of an ethereal plane,

In the alliterative dance, they entertain.

Whispering winds, weave words in rhyme,

Imaginary elements in rhythm and time,

With alliteration's art, in prose and mime,

An enchanting world, where dreams climb.

Sophia Verse

Euphonic Euphemisms of

Imaginary Elements

In the realm of euphemisms, where words embrace,

Imaginary elements find their sacred place,

With gentle euphony, their mystique we trace,

Where truth and fantasy interlace.

Whispers of euphemisms, in twilight's glow,

Unicorn's presence, we subtly bestow,

Phoenix's rebirth, in euphonic flow,

Imaginary elements, their secrets we stow.

Dragon's fiery temper, a euphemistic air,

Enchanted forests, where wonders dare,

Euphemistic elves, with mischief to spare,

Imaginary elements, in stories we declare.

So let euphemisms veil their existence,

In the hushed tones of subtle resistance,

Imaginary elements, with gentle persistence,

In euphonic euphemisms, find their subsistence.

Imaginary Elements

Walking through dreams, in the starry night,
Where unicorns roam, in the soft moonlight,
With dragons in flight, such an epic sight,
Imaginary elements, take me to new heights.

Imaginary elements, in a world so bright,
Fantasy and wonder, take flight,
Mermaids sing, in the ocean's might,
Imaginary elements, pure delight.

Through enchanted forests, we'll make our way,
With elves and fairies, where they sway,
In this world of dreams, we'll forever stay,
Imaginary elements, come what may.

Imaginary elements, in a world so bright,
Fantasy and wonder, take flight,
Unicorns gallop, in the pale moonlight,
Imaginary elements, our guiding light.

Sophia Verse

Let's sail on the back of a mythical steed,
Across the skies, where dreams exceed,
Imaginary elements, fulfill our need,
In this world of wonder, where hearts are freed.

Imaginary elements, in a world so bright,
Fantasy and wonder, take flight,
Phoenix's rebirth, in the morning light,
Imaginary elements, ignite the night.

Imaginary elements, our dreams ignite,
In this world of wonder, where stars unite,
With each verse and rhyme, we'll take flight,
Imaginary elements, in our hearts, ignite.

The Time-Stopper Sword

Walking through time, with a sword in hand,
It can stop the world, like grains of sand,
In its shimmering blade, I understand,
A time-stopper's power, in this magical land.

The Time-Stopper Sword, in my command,
Pauses the seconds, as moments expand,
With a swing so bold, I take my stand,
Time's secrets unlocked, it's so grand.

Through history's pages, I'll swiftly glide,
With the sword of ages, by my side,
In this timeless journey, we'll confide,
A world of wonder, where time can't hide.

The Time-Stopper Sword, a mystical guide,
In its gleaming hilt, the past and future collide,
With a single stroke, I'll turn the tide,
Time's mysteries unraveled, nowhere to hide.

Let's freeze the seconds, in this dance we lead,
With the sword's magic, fulfilling our need,
The Time-Stopper Sword, a powerful steed,
In this timeless adventure, our hearts freed.

The Time-Stopper Sword, our destiny decreed,
In its radiant aura, the world's secrets conceded,
With each swing and thrust, our foes impede,
Time's reign challenged, as heroes succeed.

The Time-Stopper Sword, in our hands, we heed,
A magical blade, in moments of need,
With each epic battle, we'll take the lead,
Time's march halted, as legends we breed.

The Realm of Imagination

Amidst the meadows of the mind's delight,

Where thoughts take flight in fanciful array,

There lies a realm, both boundless and bright,

Where imagination holds undying sway.

With every stroke of thought, a world anew,

In colors vivid, dreams and visions bloom,

A canvas vast, where skies of azure blue,

Reflect the wonders of the mind's perfume.

Within this realm, the poet finds his muse,

And paints with words the landscapes of the soul,

Where verses flow like rivers, swift to fuse,

Their essence pure, a tapestry unrolled.

So let us journey, poets, young and old,

Where realms of thought in endless splendor lie,

For in imagination's embrace, we're bold,

To shape the worlds that in our spirits lie.

The Journey Beneath the Sea

In a world beneath the ocean's deep,

A hobbit named Milo took a leap,

With dwarves and wizard, they set sail,

To find a treasure, a dragon's tale.

On their quest, they faced great trials,

From trolls and goblins, to riddles and miles,

With Milo's courage and Sting so bright,

They journeyed onward, through day and night.

In the heart of darkness, Smog did lie,

A fire-breathing dragon, ready to fly,

Milo, the burglar, with steps so sly,

Stole a golden cup, with a gleam in his eye.

They riddled with Glimmer, in the caverns deep,

For a chance to escape, Milo had to keep,

The One Ring hidden, a powerful prize,

A burden that would later surprise.

They battled with orcs and spiders so vile,
In the forest of Mirkwood, mile after mile,
Until they reached the Lonely Mountain's door,
Where Smog's treasure lay, a boundless store.

With courage and cunning, they faced the beast,
Smog's fiery fury, they aimed to cease,
With arrows and stones, they struck him down,
A kingdom reclaimed, a golden crown.

But greed and power, they can corrupt,
Gloin's heart grew cold, his soul disrupted,
Yet in the end, he found his way,
As friendship prevailed, in the light of day.

Back beneath the sea, Milo returned,
A wiser hobbit, his lessons learned,
With tales to tell and memories to share,
The journey beneath the sea, beyond compare.

A Quest to the Heart of Our World

In days of yore, a daring quest begun,
By Captain Harlow, a fearless, noble one,
With loyal comrades, fearless and true,
They ventured deep, where secrets grew.

Through caverns dark, where light was scarce,
They journeyed forth, with hopes to pierce,
The Earth's own heart, its core so vast,
A world within, they ventured fast.

Strange creatures met, and perils faced,
In this subterranean, hidden place,
But Captain Harlow, with wisdom and might,
Guided his crew, through day and night.

At the journey's end, a wonder revealed,
The heart of our world, its secrets unsealed,
A tale of courage, and discoveries grand,
For in exploration, they made their stand.

The Odyssey Beneath the Waves

Captain Reynard, a mariner renowned,

Set sail beneath the waves, where mysteries abound,

His vessel, The Aquanaut, a marvel of might,

Explored the deep, in the darkest night.

With a loyal crew, valiant and brave,

They journeyed through oceans, their spirits save,

Encountering leviathans, and wonders untold,

Beneath the sea's surface, their story unfolds.

Captain Reynard, a master of the deep,

With harpoon in hand, his watch he'd keep,

But in the end, a revelation they'd find,

That beneath the waves, a new world designed.

So let us hail this aquatic tale,

Of Captain Reynard and his brave travail,

For in the depths of the ocean's embrace,

They found a world, a wondrous place.

An Expedition to Earth's Core

Professor Allard, with knowledge vast,

Led an expedition, an adventure so fast,

With his niece, Lady Elara, by his side,

They delved into Earth, where wonders hide.

Through underground realms, they journeyed deep,

Where ancient mysteries, their secrets keep,

Encountering subterranean life, unknown and wild,

As they ventured forth, their spirits compiled.

Professor Allard, a man of science and lore,

With Lady Elara, whom he did adore,

Unveiled the Earth's secrets, its core they'd reach,

A journey of discovery, a remarkable speech.

So let us celebrate this epic descent,

Of Professor Allard and Lady Elara, intent,

To explore the Earth, its heart they'd find,

An expedition of intellect and mind.

Postface

Sophia Verse

Dear Reader,

As you reach the end of "Words Through AI: Poems in the Spirit of the Artificial Intelligence," we invite you to reflect on the unique journey you've just undertaken. This collection is a testament to the intersection of art and technology, where the human imagination meets the boundless capabilities of artificial intelligence.

In these pages, you've explored the creative tapestry woven by AI, inspired by the styles and voices of poets who have shaped literary history. From Shelley's romantic verses to Pope's satirical wit, from Poe's enigmatic tales to Wordsworth's transcendental musings, each poem is a testament to the power of collaboration between man and machine.

The poems you've encountered here are not mere imitations but rather a testament to the limitless possibilities of AI as a creative partner. They capture not only the essence of great poets but also the ever-relevant themes that have stirred human hearts for centuries. Love, nature, self-discovery, and the complexities of existence are threads that continue to bind us, even as we embrace the era of artificial intelligence.

This collection is a celebration of both the past and the future, where technology and human expression converge. It reminds us that, through AI, we can explore new dimensions of creativity and understanding. These poems are a bridge between the literary traditions of old and the innovations of today.

As you close this book, we hope you carry with you a sense of wonder and curiosity about the evolving landscape of literature and AI's role in shaping it. Poetry remains a timeless vessel for exploring the depths of the human experience, and now, with AI, it becomes a vessel for exploring new frontiers.

Thank you for embarking on this extraordinary journey with us. May the words you've encountered here continue to inspire, challenge, and expand your horizons as you navigate the ever-evolving world of words and artificial intelligence.

With appreciation for your exploration,

Sophia Verse

Sophia Verse

Credits

Published by entropunda in November 2023.

The cover has been designed using assets from Freepik.com.

Table of Contents

Love's Eternal Rhyme

Sea of Love's Sorrow

Love's Many Hues

A Homage to the Heart

Echoes of Love's Infinity

The Whisper of Dawn

The Storm of Passion

The Quietude of Twilight

The Pain of Separation

The Eternal Flame

The Dawn of Love

The Storm of Desire

The Labyrinth of Affection

The Eclipse of Sorrow

The Infinity of Union

The Mechanical Heart

Sonnet of Steel

Ballad of the Wired Heart

Nature and Seasons